DR. DINESH KUMAR

SHE WILL if SHE WILLS

BlueRose ONE .com
Stories Matter
NewDelhi • London

BLUEROSE PUBLISHERS
U.K.

BlueRose ONE.com
Stories Matter
NewDelhi • London

For permissions requests or inquiries regarding this publication, please contact:

BLUEROSE PUBLISHERS
www.BlueRoseONE.com
info@bluerosepublishers.com
+4407342408967

ISBN: 978-93-6783-376-6

Cover design: Daksh
Typesetting: Tanya Raj Upadhyay

First Edition: February 2025

Preface:
Awakening the Leader Within

This book is a tapestry of courage, introspection, and the unyielding spirit of women navigating personal and professional crossroads. **She Will if She Wills** is not just a story of Christy, an accomplished professional at a pivotal moment in her career, and her daughter Emily, a young woman stepping into the world of possibilities—it's a celebration of resilience and the choices that shape us.

Through a series of candid conversations and encounters, the narrative explores profound themes of ambition, sacrifice, and empowerment. From an early morning question that sparks introspection to stories of women defying odds in politics, business, and daily life, the book sheds light on the struggles and triumphs that define the journey of every woman.

The characters' realizations mirror the inner dialogues many of us have—facing self-doubt, overcoming societal expectations, and discovering untapped potential. As Christy and Emily learn to inspire themselves to inspire others, their journey becomes a guidepost for anyone striving to align their aspirations with their sense of purpose.

This book invites readers to reflect, challenge their perspectives, and embrace their own power to lead. Because sometimes, the most remarkable journeys begin with a single, conscious choice: to will it into existence.

Table of Contents

The Question

A simple question triggers a big journey

Christy stretched as she got out of bed, the soft glow of the morning sun filtering through the pale blue curtains of her bedroom. The light cast a warm, welcoming hue, one of those mornings that whispered promises of good things ahead. Yet, Christy had a hint of unease she couldn't shake off, lingering like a shadow. She brushed it aside, chalking it up to the remnants of her dream—something about missed opportunities, though she couldn't recall the details. Maybe they didn't matter. Today, after all, was another opportunity to tackle the world head-on.

She went about her routine with efficiency, slipping into the role she played so well: Christy Lawson, VP of Marketing at SnackNest. A veteran in the snacking industry, she'd become a powerhouse, known not just for her talent in developing campaigns that kept SnackNest relevant but for her rare ability to inspire. People at the company trusted her because she always delivered and, perhaps more importantly, because she listened. She was as known for her brilliant ideas as she was for her magnetic, approachable leadership style. As she applied a touch of makeup in the mirror, she thought briefly of the team meeting scheduled for later that morning. Another product launch was just around the corner, and she could feel the familiar rush of excitement start to bubble within her. It was time to get to work.

But as she made her way downstairs, she spotted Emily, her daughter, already up, sipping her coffee at the kitchen table. Emily looked thoughtful, almost too serious for a college student enjoying her morning time. Christy's heart softened. The busy pace of life often kept them from these small, quiet moments, but she knew she'd have to savor every one of them before Emily headed back to school.

"Morning, Em," Christy greeted, taking a seat across from her.

"Morning, Mom," Emily replied, looking up. Her brows were knit, the same way Christy's often were when she was deep in thought. "Can I ask you something?"

"Of course. What's on your mind?"

Emily took a breath, her fingers tracing a small circle on the table. "Why are there so few female CEOs?"

The question hit Christy like a sudden gust of wind, catching her off guard. She'd spent her career focused on climbing the ranks, proving herself worthy of each role she took on. But the issue Emily raised wasn't new to her. It was something she'd often thought about, though she rarely voiced it. The scarcity of women at the top of the corporate ladder was glaring, especially in industries like hers.

"That's...a good question," Christy finally said, her voice measured. "A very good question."

But the question stirred something deeper in her–an old, familiar tension she tried not to think about. The gap between where she was now and that elusive, final step up to the C-suite was a chasm that had lingered over her for years. She was qualified, of that she was certain. But that next level, it always seemed somehow... out of reach.

Emily tilted her head, her curiosity palpable. "You don't have to answer right now," she said, though her eyes suggested she hoped for more.

Christy smiled, a bit sadder than she intended. "Oh, trust me, I've thought about it plenty. I just don't always have the answers," she admitted, as much to herself as to her daughter.

It was a rare admission, but it felt good to say it aloud, to recognize that even someone as high up as she was still searching for answers. Christy wondered how many others felt this same way, caught in the in-between. It was one thing to work for a company; it was another thing entirely to sit at the top and truly shape it. But could she make that leap?

She let the question linger in her mind as she poured herself a coffee, the steam curling up into the quiet morning air. While the question rattled around, she thought about the obstacles she'd already overcome—the late nights, the countless pitches, the endless meetings where she'd had to work twice as hard to be taken seriously. She'd spent her entire career demonstrating that she could perform at the top levels, often exceeding her male counterparts. So, what was missing?

A soft sigh escaped her lips, pulling Emily's gaze back to her. "You know, Em, the world's changing. More women are moving into those roles, even if it's slower than we'd like. But it's not always about talent or experience. Sometimes… well, sometimes it's about the perception of who belongs in that role."

Emily leaned forward, her eyes wide. "But… if it's just about perception, why does it matter? Shouldn't the results speak for themselves?"

Christy smiled at her daughter's simplicity, her own words echoing in her head from years ago. She thought back to when she was Emily's age, with her own ideas about how she'd blaze her path. How clear it all had seemed back then.

"In an ideal world, yes. But the reality is, breaking those perceptions takes time. It means changing minds, showing people what women can accomplish when they're given a chance. That's why every step forward matters, even if it's one person at a time." She placed her hand on Emily's. "And it means not giving up when it feels like the odds are stacked against you."

Emily's face softened, though her eyes held a spark of determination. "So, you're saying you still want that job? CEO?"

Christy laughed, surprised. "Why not? I've come this far. But it's a process, Em. I'll get there when the time is right."

Emily studied her mother's face, nodding slowly. "Then I'm sure you will, Mom."

Christy squeezed her daughter's hand, a swell of pride filling her chest. "Thanks, Em. Now, I need to get going. Big day ahead."

With one last glance at her daughter, she straightened her shoulders and turned toward the door, the morning light spilling across her determined face. She wasn't just heading to work; she was heading toward her future, knowing that with each step, she was one stride closer to claiming her place at the top. The path might be hard, but Christy Lawson had always thrived under pressure. And as the door clicked shut behind her, she felt a renewed sense of purpose she hadn't felt in a long time.

"Sometimes we need an awakening. No matter where it comes from."

The Daughter's Insight

Emily's anxiety fuels Christy's curiosity

Emily sat alone at the kitchen table, her mom's words still echoing in her mind. She swirled her coffee absently, her gaze fixed somewhere beyond the rim of her cup. How could Christy think that becoming CEO was about "the right time"? If anyone was ready, it was her mother. She'd watched her for years, managing the family, juggling work and home with a calm, unshakeable confidence that Emily could only dream of. Her mother was resilient, disciplined, and above all, committed. But there was a quiet strength about Christy, too, a kind of steady fire that never wavered, even when things went wrong.

Emily couldn't help but admire her. She remembered late nights when Christy had stayed up with her, helping with school projects or calming her worries over college applications, even after coming home from a long day at the office. And somehow, Christy still managed to lead her team, launch products, and maintain her position in an industry that Emily knew was dominated by men. All without missing a beat.

But there was something else, something her mother hadn't said outright. Emily felt it simmering just beneath Christy's calm words earlier that morning. *Perception.* That single word had lingered in

Emily's mind. Was that really all that kept women like her mother from reaching the top?

Emily shook her head, unable to let it go. She picked up her phone, her fingers hovering over the screen. Her mother would be at the office by now, already neck-deep in meetings, decisions, and plans. But Emily needed to talk to her. This wasn't just some passing thought–this was the realization that the person she looked up to, the person she believed in, was somehow held back. It felt unfair. And if there was one thing Emily had inherited from Christy, it was her determination to get answers.

She tapped the screen, dialing her mother's number. After a couple of rings, Christy picked up.

"Hey, Em. Is everything okay?" Christy's voice came through, warm but a little distracted.

"Yeah, yeah, everything's fine. Are you in the middle of something?" Emily asked, a touch of hesitation in her voice.

Christy chuckled softly. "I've got a minute. What's on your mind?"

Emily hesitated, gathering her thoughts. "Mom, I just... I can't stop thinking about what we talked about this morning. About CEOs, women in leadership... all of that."

There was a brief pause before Christy replied. "It's a lot to think about, isn't it?"

"It is," Emily said, pressing on. "I mean, look at you. You're already doing everything a CEO would. You lead a whole team, you manage multiple projects, you solve problems... You're already practically running the place! Why aren't you CEO?"

The line went quiet. Christy's silence was thoughtful, maybe even a little tense. Emily could feel the weight of the unspoken words.

"You're sweet, Em. But it's not as simple as just doing the job well. It's about a hundred little things, things you wouldn't even imagine," Christy replied carefully.

"But those little things..." Emily pushed, her voice growing more intense. "Why should they matter? Isn't it enough that you're good at what you do?"

Christy sighed, her voice softening. "I know it sounds strange. But there are still... expectations, people who make decisions based on things that have nothing to do with talent or capability. It's frustrating, but it's real. And it's something I'm still working through, still trying to navigate."

"Working through?" Emily's eyebrows shot up. "Mom, if you're still working through it, then what does that mean for the rest of us? Women my age, who are just starting out? What do we have to do?"

Christy laughed gently, but Emily could hear the hint of sadness beneath it. "Oh, Em. If there's one thing I've learned, it's that the rules are always changing. Every generation faces new challenges, new perceptions to break down. But what you have to remember is that it's not impossible. It just takes persistence."

Emily's chest tightened as she listened. She wanted to believe her mother, to hold on to the idea that with enough effort, she could reach any position, any title she wanted. But the thought of how long it might take, of the unseen obstacles in her path, made her stomach twist.

"You know what, Mom?" Emily said, a spark of determination igniting in her chest. "You don't have to wait for the 'right time.' You already have everything it takes. Why not go for it now?"

Christy chuckled softly. "You really think so?"

"Yes! I mean it, Mom. You've always taught me that if you believe in something, you should go after it. Well, I believe in you. And I know you believe in yourself, too."

There was a long pause, and Emily could almost picture her mother leaning back in her office chair, gazing out her window, lost in thought. She knew her mom was strong, but she also knew Christy was human. The constant push, the endless uphill climb—it took its toll.

Finally, Christy spoke, her voice steady, but with a hint of something Emily hadn't heard before: resolve. "You know what, Em? Maybe you're right. Maybe I have been waiting when I should've been acting."

Emily's heart skipped a beat. "So... you'll go for it?"

A slight laugh came through the phone, one that felt lighter, freer. "I don't know what that looks like just yet, but yes. Maybe it's time I start looking at things differently, and... taking a few risks."

Emily beamed, her own excitement bubbling over. "Yes! That's what I'm talking about!"

"Thank you, Em. I didn't realize how much I needed to hear this," Christy said, her voice touched with gratitude. "You're right, you know. Sometimes, even the strongest need a push."

They hung up, and as Emily sat back, a new sense of pride settled over her. It wasn't often that she got to inspire her mom. But for the first time, Emily felt like she'd sparked something. Christy had always been the source of her strength, her confidence, but now, in her own small way, Emily had given something back.

And as she glanced at the empty coffee cup on the table, she couldn't help but feel that the conversation wasn't just about her mother's journey–it was about her own. For the first time, she saw a glimpse of her future, the road she would one day have to travel. And while it was filled with unknowns, she knew one thing for sure: she was ready to face it.

Little did Emily know; this was only the beginning. The quiet push she'd given her mother was about to set off a chain of events that neither of them could have foreseen.

"Perceptions can be managed never allow them to beat you down.

Cab Driver's Wisdom

It is never easy for a single mom

Emily glanced at her phone, eyes widening as she realized how much time had slipped by. *I'm going to miss the bus.* She grabbed her bag, sprinted down the steps, and dashed outside. The early morning rush was already beginning, and her usual bus had long disappeared down the road.

Guess it's a cab today, she thought, pulling up the app to request one. Within minutes, a silver car pulled up beside her. She slid into the back seat and glanced at the driver, surprised to see a woman behind the wheel—a rare sight in their city.

"Morning," Emily greeted as she buckled in.

"Good morning," the driver replied, her eyes warm in the rearview mirror. She was older, in her mid-40s perhaps, with silver-streaked hair tied back in a ponytail and a calm, sturdy presence. Her name flashed on Emily's app screen: *Helga*.

The drive was quiet at first, with only the soft hum of the engine filling the silence. Emily, still processing her conversation with her mother, found herself drifting back into her thoughts. But a few minutes into the ride, Helga glanced at her phone, her expression shifting as it buzzed.

"Do you mind if I pull over for a moment?" she asked, catching Emily's eyes in the mirror. "I need to take a call from my son."

"Oh, of course! Go ahead." Emily nodded, a bit surprised but curious.

Helga pulled over and took the call, her face breaking into a smile as she spoke, her voice soft and warm. When she ended the call, she put her phone down and let out a small, contented sigh.

"Everything okay?" Emily asked, intrigued.

"Yes, better than okay," Helga said, her tone proud. "My son's graduating this weekend. I'll be attending his ceremony."

"That's wonderful! Congratulations," Emily replied, sensing there was more to the story.

Helga's eyes sparkled as she glanced back at Emily. "Thank you. I'm very proud of him. He's come a long way... we both have, actually."

Emily leaned forward, sensing a story worth hearing. "I'd love to hear about it, if you don't mind sharing."

Helga smiled, adjusting her grip on the wheel as they pulled back into traffic. "Well, let's see... my husband passed away when my son was just ten years old. He was my whole world, and when he was gone, I felt lost. I hadn't worked a day in my life. I didn't know how I'd support my son or give him the future I wanted for him."

Emily's heart tightened as she listened, imagining how terrifying that must have been.

"It took me some time, but I realized I didn't have a choice. I had to find a way to make it work. I tried a few jobs, but none of them gave me the flexibility I needed. My son needed me around, and I needed to be able to provide for him without being gone all day."

"So... you chose cab driving?" Emily guessed, her curiosity growing.

"Yes," Helga nodded, smiling at the memory. "I know it sounds unusual, but it worked. Driving allowed me to set my own hours, to be there for him when he needed me. And I didn't have to rely on anyone. Every day I drove, every fare I earned, I knew I was building a better future for both of us."

Emily felt a swell of admiration. "That must've taken a lot of courage."

Helga glanced at her in the mirror, a glimmer of determination in her eyes. "Courage, determination... a lot of things I didn't even know I had. And I realized something important along the way."

"What's that?"

Helga's smile grew, touched with both pride and regret. "I realized that I could have done this even when my husband was alive. I'd let myself depend on him, thinking that was just how things were meant to be. But I didn't need to wait. We women are capable of so much more than we often believe."

Emily felt something shift inside her, a new awareness unfolding like the first rays of dawn. *I could have done this even when my husband was alive.* Helga's words lingered in her mind, resonating deeply. For years, Emily had watched her mother push through obstacles, balancing everything with grace. But here was another woman, another kind of role model, showing her that sometimes life pushed you before you realized how much you were capable of.

"So, what kept you going?" Emily asked, genuinely curious. "There must have been times when you thought about giving up."

"Oh, plenty of times," Helga admitted, a small laugh escaping her. "There were days I was exhausted, or when customers were rude, or when I just missed my husband too much. But every time I thought about giving up, I reminded myself of my goal—to see my son graduate, to make him proud. I had to be strong, not just for me, but for him. I had to show him that even when life knocks you down, you can get back up."

Emily's heart swelled with respect. "You're amazing, you know that?"

Helga chuckled, her eyes crinkling with warmth. "Thank you. But I think a lot of us have it in us. We just have to find the right reasons to bring it out."

They rode in comfortable silence for a few moments, Emily absorbing everything she'd just heard. A thought began to form, something she hadn't fully considered before. She had always seen her mother as this invincible figure, someone who balanced everything with ease. But maybe it wasn't about balancing everything perfectly—maybe it was about being willing to push, to risk, to keep moving forward, even when things felt impossible.

"I think you're right," Emily said finally. "Women shouldn't have to wait for someone to tell them they're ready. We have to be ready for ourselves."

Helga nodded, her voice strong and full of conviction. "Exactly. Don't wait for the world to catch up to you. If you have a dream, if there's something you want to achieve, go after it. Set your own goals, and then make them happen. Because you can. You'd be amazed at what you're capable of when you just take that first step."

As the cab pulled up in front of Emily's college, she felt a new surge of determination she hadn't expected to find today. She glanced at Helga with gratitude, feeling as if she'd just unlocked a new layer of herself.

"Thank you, Helga. Really," she said as she gathered her things. "You've given me a lot to think about."

Helga smiled, her eyes shining with understanding. "Remember, Emily–don't be afraid to push yourself. You're stronger than you think."

Emily nodded, stepping out of the cab and closing the door behind her. She watched Helga drive off, her heart thudding with a new sense of purpose. Helga's story had given her a different perspective, one that her mother had begun to hint at but that only now made sense. She couldn't rely on the world to open doors for her; she had to be the one to turn the knob.

As she walked toward her class, Emily knew that something had shifted inside her. She wasn't just a college student anymore; she was someone with a goal, someone who understood that her journey, just like her mother's and Helga's, was hers to shape.

And maybe–just maybe–it was time to set her sights higher than she'd ever thought possible.

Courage and Determination is all it takes not just to face life's challenges but to keep surging ahead

Pregnant Colleague's Perspective

Family or work? Doesn't have to be either or

Christy breezed through her work that day with a speed and clarity she hadn't felt in years. It was as if a weight had lifted, and in its place was a sharp, clear focus. Task after task fell into place, her mind working with a new, quiet confidence. There was something invigorating about the morning's conversation with Emily, something that felt like a spark kindling deep inside her.

She glanced at the clock and decided it was time for a well-earned break. Rising from her desk, she headed to the cafeteria, craving both coffee and a moment to reflect on what lay ahead. As she stepped into the bustling room, she spotted Mia standing by the counter, her hand resting on her growing belly. Mia, in her seventh month of pregnancy, was one of the company's rising stars—a sharp, driven project manager who seemed to have boundless energy, even now.

"Mia!" Christy called out, smiling as she walked over.

Mia's face lit up. "Christy! How are you?"

"Oh, I'm good. Needed a break—feels like it's been non-stop since morning. How about you?"

Christy's gaze drifted briefly to Mia's stomach. "How's the little one?"

Mia beamed, resting her hand gently on her belly. "Growing more every day. I think he'll be kicking his way into the world soon enough." She laughed, then added, "I can't believe I'm already in my third trimester. It feels like just yesterday I was worrying about managing my team and a baby at the same time."

Christy smiled warmly. "Well, from what I've seen, you're doing a phenomenal job. I don't know how you're managing it all—pregnancy, work, everything."

Mia shrugged, a proud glint in her eye. "It's not always easy, but I had a plan, you know? I made sure I had a roadmap for both my career and motherhood. I knew that I didn't want either one to get in the way of the other."

Christy raised an eyebrow, intrigued. "A roadmap? Tell me more about that. I think I could have used one when I was your age."

Mia chuckled. "Well, the way I see it, being a mother and becoming a leader are both really important to me. It's about priorities. I sat down with my manager and made a plan for my maternity leave, making sure there was a clear handover and support for my team while I'm away. And I also worked out a phased return. I know it won't be easy, but I wanted to make sure I didn't lose momentum just because I'm taking time off."

Christy nodded, a pang of admiration and maybe even a touch of envy hitting her. "I admire that kind of clarity, Mia. You're not treating it as an either-or decision."

Mia's face softened. "No, because it doesn't have to be. Women so often feel that they need to choose between their family and their careers. But I'm determined to prove, at least to myself, that I can succeed at both. It takes planning, it takes support, but it's possible. And I want to set that example–not just for my son, but for every woman who feels like they have to choose."

Christy felt a deep surge of respect for this young woman standing in front of her. In many ways, she saw a version of herself–ambitious, hopeful, but without the clarity and confidence Mia seemed to have. When she'd started her family, she'd felt pulled in a dozen directions, unsure if she could have it all, and always doubting whether she was doing enough for her career or for Emily. But here was Mia, mapping out her path with courage and conviction.

"You know, Mia, I wish I'd met someone like you twenty years ago," Christy admitted, her tone thoughtful. "I think it would've made a difference."

Mia looked at her, a glint of warmth in her eyes. "Well, it's never too late, Christy. From what I hear, you've been an incredible leader here. I know you're someone who has a huge impact on everyone who works with you. Maybe now's the time for you to set your sights even higher."

Christy's heart skipped a beat. *Set your sights even higher.* The words settled over her like a calling. She was already well-respected, experienced, and had the confidence of her team. Why not take that final leap? Why not strive for the role she'd always quietly dreamed about?

"What you're saying..." Christy began, choosing her words carefully. "It's exactly what my daughter and I were discussing this morning. She asked me why there are so few female CEOs in the world. I told her it's complicated, that sometimes it's about waiting for the right time. But now, after speaking with her, and listening to you–I'm starting to wonder if maybe I've been waiting too long."

Mia nodded, her gaze unwavering. "Christy, don't wait for anyone to tell you it's time. If you want it, go after it. You're more than qualified. You just need to believe that it's yours to take."

Christy took a deep breath, feeling an incredible surge of strength and certainty wash over her. "You're right," she said, her voice resolute. "I don't need to wait anymore. I'm going for it."

They shared a quiet smile, one of mutual respect and shared understanding. For Christy, this conversation with Mia felt like the final piece of a puzzle falling into place. This was more than just a goal–it was about setting a standard, about showing women like Mia and Emily that it was possible to lead, to inspire, and to succeed without sacrificing the things that mattered most.

As they walked back to their respective offices, Christy felt a renewed sense of purpose. She wasn't just doing this for herself. She was doing it for every woman who looked up to her, who saw her journey as a road map for their own.

And as she glanced back at Mia, she realized that this wasn't just the start of her own journey. It was the start of something bigger, something that could change the way women viewed their place in the corporate world. For the first time in years, she felt certain that she was exactly where she needed to be.

This time, she thought, *I'm not holding back.*

Decision making is the key, be it family or work and at times even more important to take both along

Unsung Heroes

Silent Performer Speaks Up

Christy returned to her desk, her mind still humming from her conversation with Mia. She felt electrified, as if a fire had been reignited inside her. Taking a deep breath, she allowed herself a moment of reflection before diving back into her work. Her office had a glass door that faced the atrium, offering a panoramic view of the building's ground floor. It was there, just below her, that she noticed Clara standing in the middle of her team, a familiar figure exuding calm authority as she addressed her staff.

Clara. Christy couldn’t help but smile as she observed the scene. In the ten years Clara had been with SnackNest, she'd gone from working in housekeeping to becoming the facilities manager, responsible for the entire building. She was a symbol of resilience and hard work, of overcoming odds without sacrificing dignity or integrity.

Christy recalled a conversation she’d had with Clara a few years ago, back when Clara was still managing cleaning crews and yet speaking with clear, unshakable ambition. Clara had shared her goal with Christy that day, her eyes focused with a determination that left an impression. "I’m going to be a manager someday," Clara had said firmly, her voice ringing with conviction. "It won’t be easy, but

I'll make it happen. Not by seeking anyone's approval, just through hard work."

And she had. Clara had never seemed bothered by what others thought or how people viewed her job in housekeeping. She was there every day, consistent and humble, focusing only on getting the work done to the best of her ability. Watching her now, Christy felt a deep respect for Clara's journey.

Unable to resist, she grabbed her phone and headed down to the ground floor. As she approached, Clara looked up, her eyes lighting up with surprise.

"Christy! What brings you down here?" Clara greeted her with a warm smile, extending a hand but then leaning in for a quick hug instead.

"I just wanted to say hello," Christy replied, smiling back. "I was watching you up there, seeing you lead your team. You looked so confident and strong. I couldn't help but think back to when we first met."

Clara chuckled, her eyes sparkling with humility. "It's been a journey, that's for sure. But I wouldn't trade it for anything. I learned so much on the way up, things that made me stronger and, hopefully, wiser."

Christy nodded thoughtfully. “I remember that conversation we had, years ago. You told me you’d make it here. And here you are, exactly where you said you’d be.”

Clara’s smile was steady, filled with pride, yet still laced with her signature modesty. “Yes, but I knew it would take time. You can’t rush these things, you know? It’s like you plant a seed, but you have to keep tending to it every day. Watering it, feeding it. It doesn’t matter if anyone else is watching. You do it because that’s what it takes to grow.”

Christy felt a surge of admiration. “And you did it all without letting other people’s opinions or judgments get to you.”

Clara shrugged, her expression one of quiet strength. “Oh, people had plenty of opinions, believe me. There were times they’d look at me like I didn’t belong, or that I was too ambitious for someone in housekeeping. But those opinions... they don’t feed you. They don’t get the work done. I always knew that if I let those voices hold me back, I’d never make it anywhere.”

Christy felt a deep resonance with her words. "That’s powerful, Clara. It’s easy to let other people’s perceptions shape the way we think about ourselves.

But you, you just stayed focused on the work and let that speak for you."

"Exactly," Clara replied, her voice calm yet brimming with pride. "There's a lot of power in hard work, in just putting your head down and doing the best job you can. But I'll tell you something else I've learned, too. As I climbed up, I realized it's okay to feel proud of where you are, so long as you stay humble. I'm proud of what I've accomplished, but I know there's always more to learn."

Christy took a deep breath, feeling a renewed sense of clarity from Clara's words. *Pride and humility,* she thought. *Those are the marks of a true leader.*

They stood in comfortable silence for a moment, watching the atrium buzz with activity. The teams were moving in and out, and the hum of productivity filled the space around them.

"Clara, you've got something special, you know that?" Christy said, her voice sincere. "You're showing everyone that there are no limits to where you can go, no matter where you start. I wish I'd learned that lesson a long time ago."

Clara laughed softly. "Well, better late than never, right? And I have a feeling you're ready to go even higher than you already are, Christy."

The words struck Christy like a bolt of lightning. There was a wisdom to Clara, a confidence that reminded her of what she herself was capable of. Christy had always been a natural leader, but somewhere along the way, she'd let doubts and insecurities creep in, wondering if the leap to CEO was too big or too ambitious. But here was Clara, someone who had risen from the ground up, standing before her as a reminder that titles were not given—they were earned.

Christy smiled, feeling a surge of energy. "You know, Clara, I think you're right. It's time for me to go for it."

Clara's smile widened, her face full of encouragement. "Then do it. You've already shown us all what you're capable of, Christy. You're already a leader. Now go and show them that you're meant to lead even more."

Christy nodded, her heart pounding with a newfound resolve. She felt more than ready—she felt destined for it. And as she made her way back to her office, Clara's words echoed in her mind, affirming her choice, strengthening her resolve.

With every step, she knew she wasn't walking back to just another day at work. She was walking toward the future she'd been building all along, a future that, at last, she felt truly ready to seize.

To be proud and humble at the same time is a great leadership quality

White Paper Lessons

A simple presentation leads to a great life experience

Good morning, Mrs. Paul!" Emily greeted cheerfully as she entered the college hallway, her steps brisk as she hurried toward the Economics classroom.

"Good morning, Em," replied Professor Alice Paul with a small smile. Her tone had a hint of mystery, a slight gleam in her eyes. "Hope you're prepared and ready."

Emily's stomach dropped. *Prepared and ready? For what?* In a flash, it hit her–she was supposed to present her white paper on macroeconomics today. Her heart skipped a beat as she realized how her conversation with her mother, Christy, had dominated her thoughts all morning. She'd been so absorbed in questions of leadership and ambition that she'd almost forgotten her own immediate goal.

"Oh, yes, of course, Mrs. Paul," she managed, keeping her voice steady. Deep down, though, she felt the nervous flutter of having been caught off guard. But she knew she'd prepared well for this. She'd spent countless hours polishing her presentation, refining her points, making sure every element was solid. She just needed to push past the distraction and focus.

This is just another moment, she told herself. *How many times in life do personal issues intrude, threatening to throw you off track?* For women, she'd come to understand, the obstacles often seemed endless. But wasn't it a choice, in the end? To stay on course, or to let something derail you?

Emily took a deep breath, smoothing her blouse as she walked toward the front of the classroom, feeling a calm settle over her. She'd seen her mother navigate challenges with poise–she could do the same. She faced the room, meeting the eyes of her peers, and began.

Her voice grew stronger with each word, her confidence bolstered as she moved through the key points of her paper: economic cycles, policy interventions, the balance of supply and demand. She could see the attentive expressions of her classmates, a few of them even nodding along. She finished her presentation, took a steadying breath, and looked over at Mrs. Paul, who had been watching her closely with an inscrutable expression.

As the classroom filed out after the presentation, Emily walked over to Mrs. Paul, eager yet nervous. "So...how was it?" she asked, keeping her tone light but feeling her heartbeat quicken.

Mrs. Paul tilted her head slightly, studying her with a kind but searching gaze. "What do *you* think?"

Emily paused, feeling her professor's question sink in. She knew she'd done well, but there had been places she could've pushed deeper, places where her focus had slipped just slightly. "I think I did well," she answered honestly, "but I could have been better."

Mrs. Paul's face broke into a warm smile. "Good. Now that you can see that yourself, I'm certain you'll do even better next time. Self-awareness is one of the most valuable qualities you can have."

Emily felt a surge of pride mixed with relief. She'd expected straightforward feedback, but instead, Mrs. Paul was giving her something more valuable: a lesson.

"There's a fine line between confidence and overconfidence, Em," Mrs. Paul continued. "Self-introspection, being able to look at your own performance with a critical eye—that's the mark of real leadership. And seeking feedback is only as valuable as your willingness to accept it."

Emily nodded, taking in her words. There was a humbling power in accepting feedback, in seeing her own work through someone else's lens. She felt her confidence grow–not in a boastful way, but in a steady, grounded sense that this was part of her journey.

"Thank you, Mrs. Paul," Emily said, feeling a spark of new understanding settle within her. "I think... I needed that reminder."

Mrs. Paul nodded knowingly. "We all need it from time to time. Just remember, the greatest leaders are the ones who never stop learning. That's how they stay grounded."

Emily left the classroom, her mind abuzz with the impact of Mrs. Paul's words. As she walked through the hallways, she couldn't help but reflect on how this morning had unfolded. Her mother's journey, Clara's resilience, Mia's careful planning–they were all so different, yet each woman had carved a path forward despite personal obstacles. And now, here was Mrs. Paul, her quiet strength adding another layer to the lesson.

There was more to success than outward confidence; it was about seeking knowledge, being willing to learn, and letting feedback sharpen you rather than dim your light. As Emily walked down the hallway toward her next class, she felt a newfound certainty growing within her.

This time, it was more than just confidence–it was purpose.

As Emily slipped out of the classroom, her mind buzzed with a new clarity. When she'd first started working on that white paper, she'd seen it as just another exercise, a way to tick off credits and edge closer to her degree. Now, however, after Mrs. Paul's words, she felt the meaning behind the assignment shift into sharper focus. This paper wasn't just a task to complete; it was an opportunity to build something more enduring within herself.

Research, articulation, query handling... she thought, walking slowly down the hall toward her next class. Each skill had its place, its part in shaping her into someone capable of facing complex situations. The project hadn't just taught her about macroeconomics–it had been a subtle lesson in confidence and perseverance. Mrs. Paul had been instrumental in helping her see it. She was more than just an economics professor. She was, Emily realized, a true leader.

That's what leaders do, Emily thought, a warm admiration for Mrs. Paul flooding through her. *They help people see the purpose behind what they're doing and push them to reach for something higher.*

Her thoughts were interrupted by the familiar sound of her friend Luna's voice as he called out, "Em! How'd it go? I saw you up there giving that presentation." She jogged over, a bright grin on her face.

Emily smiled back. "It went... well, I think. Better than I'd expected. Mrs. Paul asked me afterward how I thought I did, and it really made me reflect. I think I learned more from her one question than from all the prep I did."

"Yeah? What did she say?" Luna's eyes were bright with curiosity.

Emily leaned against the wall, thoughtful. "She asked me how I thought I'd done, and when I said I could have done better, she agreed but in the kindest way. She said self-reflection and seeking feedback are essential. Made me realize this whole paper was never just about economics. It was about developing the skills I'll actually need later on."

"Wow, Mrs. Paul's got that Jedi wisdom, huh?" Luna chuckled, but her tone held respect. "That's cool, though. So you feel like it was worth the work?"

Emily's gaze grew distant for a moment. "Yeah... more than I realized at first. I was so focused on just getting the paper done that I didn't see the bigger purpose. And isn't that what being a leader is? Seeing the purpose, but also helping your team see it too? I don't know... I never really thought of Mrs. Paul that way, but now I can't unsee it."

Luna gave a slow nod. "Makes sense. The best leaders get people to see things they might've missed otherwise. Like, seeing all those steps that add up to something huge in the end."

Emily laughed softly. "Exactly. I guess it's something my mom's been trying to teach me too. She was saying the same thing this morning, that there's always a larger reason behind what we do, even if we don't see it right away. Honestly, between her and Mrs. Paul, I feel like I'm getting a crash course in leadership without even realizing it."

They both laughed, and then Luna's expression grew serious. "So... do you think you want to be a leader one day?"

Emily's smile faltered for a second, and she felt a ripple of uncertainty, followed by a spark of resolve. "Maybe. I mean, the thought of it scares me a little. There's so much responsibility, so much you have to keep sight of, but... if I can keep learning from people like Mrs. Paul and my mom, maybe one day I could be."

Luna grinned. "I'll be there cheering you on, no question about it."

They exchanged a quick, encouraging glance, and Emily turned toward her next classroom, feeling a surge of excitement. She carried the weight of Mrs. Paul's words with her, feeling almost as if she'd been given a roadmap–one that could lead her toward the future she'd only begun to dream about.

As she walked through the door, a quiet determination settled over her. Mrs. Paul's voice echoed in her mind:

The greatest leaders never stop learning.

Learning always leads to Growth

The Political Encounter

Politician's guidance to navigate corporate politics

The city was already humming with the low buzz of evening activity by the time Christy left her office, the last traces of sunlight fading as she hurried through the bustling downtown streets. Tonight wasn't just another social event on her calendar; it was the annual fundraiser for *Hope for Tomorrow*, the NGO she'd worked with for nearly a decade. The organization was more than just a volunteer commitment–it was a passion project, a place where her energy and heart collided to create something meaningful.

As she entered the event hall, Christy took a moment to observe the warm, vibrant room filled with people she'd come to know and respect. Hope for Tomorrow had transformed lives–abandoned children had found homes, guidance, education, and even employment through the relentless efforts of people like her, who dedicated not only resources but their time and expertise. She felt a surge of pride as she spotted several young people she'd once mentored, now volunteers themselves, working the tables and ushering guests to their seats.

She glanced at the stage where a podium stood, waiting for the evening's speaker, Senator Gabriela Ramirez. Christy had heard much about Senator

Ramirez's tenacity and commitment to social issues, especially those impacting women and children. The senator was known for her bold stances and her ability to cut through political noise to make a difference–an inspiration, much like Mrs. Paul or her mother had been, but in a whole new sphere. Christy couldn't wait to meet her.

The hum of chatter quieted as the event's host took the microphone, introducing Senator Ramirez with a voice full of respect and anticipation. As the senator approached the podium, she radiated a calm but powerful presence. Her gaze swept across the room, and her voice, low and commanding, filled the hall as she spoke.

"Thank you, Hope for Tomorrow, for the remarkable work you do. The world isn't always kind to those who need it most. I have seen firsthand the challenges that vulnerable children face and the impact a single act of kindness can have in transforming lives. Tonight, it's not just about raising funds; it's about creating futures, building resilience, and proving that everyone here has a role in making our society whole."

The senator's words were electric, each one landing with a precision that sent murmurs of agreement and even a few applause breaks throughout the audience. Christy watched, feeling her own heart lift with the energy of the crowd. This was exactly why she volunteered, why she spent long hours mentoring, guiding, and connecting these kids to opportunities. It was work that might not make headlines but would change lives.

Senator Ramirez concluded her speech with a promise. "I assure you, the government is committed to supporting initiatives like this. We will do more. We have to do more. And to all of you who are here tonight," she continued, her eyes scanning the room, "thank you. Your work matters."

As the applause roared through the hall, Christy felt the senator's words sink into her, echoing her own hopes for the children she had come to care for so deeply. After the speech, as dinner was served, she was delighted when she got the chance to meet the senator face-to-face.

"Senator Ramirez," Christy greeted her, a warm smile spreading across her face as she extended her hand. "Your speech was incredibly inspiring. I can't tell you how grateful we all are for your support."

The senator smiled, her handshake firm and confident. "Thank you, Christy. I'm just as inspired to meet people like you, who are out there doing the work every day. They told me about your role in the organization, and I have to say, I'm impressed." Her gaze softened, a spark of curiosity lighting her eyes. "A VP at SnackNest, a mother, and a dedicated volunteer–how do you manage it all?"

Christy laughed lightly, a bit flustered. "Well, I won't lie, it's a balancing act. But this work means the world to me. It's about making sure the next generation has something to hold onto, something to guide them. And in a way, it helps keep me grounded, too."

Senator Ramirez nodded thoughtfully. "I completely understand that. When I first entered politics, I faced some resistance, and not just from other politicians. The hurdles were everywhere. It's hard when you're told you don't belong somewhere, that you can't balance all that's expected of you. But I learned that resilience is everything. People will try to test you, but that's when you push forward. You either own your space or lose it."

Christy felt the weight of those words. "That's incredible advice. I've had my share of challenges, too. Sometimes I wonder if I'm doing enough or if I should be trying harder. But hearing you say that, I feel... encouraged."

Ramirez's expression turned resolute. "Christy, the power of influence is real, and don't underestimate what you're doing here. Whether it's in the boardroom or right here at Hope for Tomorrow, you're setting an example, just as I try to do in politics. It's all interconnected. In the end, our ability to lead comes down to what we're willing to fight for and the people we're willing to bring up with us."

Christy felt a rush of gratitude. Here was someone who understood, who had lived through similar battles and emerged stronger. Ramirez's story of resilience reminded her of all the women who had inspired her—Mrs. Paul, Clara, her mother—and each had contributed to her understanding of leadership and purpose.

"I'll remember that, Senator," Christy said, a newfound determination glinting in her eyes. "Thank you."

The senator smiled, reaching over to place a reassuring hand on her shoulder. "You're already doing more than you know. And one day, when you're ready, you'll lead others too. Keep pushing forward, Christy."

As the senator turned to greet other guests, Christy felt a profound sense of clarity. This conversation had shifted something within her. The power of influence, the importance of lifting others as she climbed–it was exactly what she wanted to embody, not just at work or with her family, but here at Hope for Tomorrow, and in every other aspect of her life.

With renewed purpose, she looked around the room, her eyes falling on the young volunteers, the kids she'd helped, and the team that made it all happen. Ramirez's words were like a spark, one that lit a fire she knew she would carry with her. She was ready to keep pushing forward, ready to lead, not just for herself, but for everyone who needed her to. And, she realized with a smile, this was only the beginning.

Hard work coupled with resilience makes you unbeatable

Grandma's Advice

Granddaughter gets a great gift – Secret to Life

The late afternoon sunbathed the retirement home in golden hues as Emily's cab pulled into the parking lot. Her phone buzzed—a text from her mom, Christy. *Take your time with Grandma. Let me know how it goes.* Emily smiled and tucked the phone away, her heart warm from the supportive message.

The home was quiet, save for the soft murmur of conversations and the occasional rustle of leaves outside the window. Ava, her grandmother, was seated on the patio, a crochet hook in one hand and a ball of yarn in the other. Her silver hair shimmered in the light, and her eyes, though weathered with age, held a lively sparkle.

"Grandma!" Emily called out, waving as she approached.

Ava looked up, her face breaking into a broad smile. "Emily, my darling! Come here and give me a hug."

After an embrace that felt like home, Emily sat down beside her. She hesitated for a moment, unsure how to broach the subject that had been on her mind since this morning's conversation with her mother.

"I hope I'm not interrupting your crochet masterpiece," Emily teased, eyeing the half-formed scarf.

"Oh, this?" Ava waved dismissively. "Just a way to keep my hands busy. Now, what brings you here today? Not that I'm complaining–seeing you is always the highlight of my week."

Emily chuckled but then grew serious. "Actually, I wanted to talk to you about something... about your career, your choices, and how you balanced everything."

Ava's smile softened, and she set the crochet aside. "Ah, so you've been talking to your mother. I had a feeling she'd send you my way sooner or later."

Emily nodded, leaning forward. "I just... I've been thinking a lot about how women navigate their careers and families. Mom's amazing at it, but I know it's not easy. And I wondered about you–how you made your decisions and what you learned from them."

Ava leaned back in her chair, her gaze drifting toward the horizon as if searching through the years for the right place to begin. "You know, Emily, when I was your age, I was full of aspirations. I wanted to do it all–climb the corporate ladder, make a name for myself. I was a young woman with big dreams, just like you."

"What happened?" Emily asked softly, sensing a deeper story.

Ava smiled wistfully. "Life happened. I worked as a junior administrator under a manager named John–an incredible mentor. He saw my potential and encouraged me to pursue bigger roles, gave me guidance on how to rise in the ranks. But back then, I wasn't sure I could handle it all. I assumed–wrongly, mind you–that a career like that would mean sacrificing my family. And when I married your grandfather, Bill, and we had your mom, I felt that my place was with them."

"Grandpa supported you, though, didn't he?" Emily asked, remembering the stories her mother had shared about her grandparents.

"Oh, absolutely," Ava said, her eyes lighting up. "Bill was my biggest cheerleader. He would've done anything to help me balance it all, but the truth is, it wasn't him holding me back–it was me. I doubted myself, doubted that I could juggle everything without dropping the ball. So, I made a choice."

Emily tilted her head. "Do you regret it?"

Ava shook her head firmly. "Not one bit. Raising your mom, watching her grow into the incredible woman she is today, and now seeing you–I wouldn't trade that for the world. But I do wonder, sometimes, what might have been if I'd pushed myself more, if I'd taken those steps John encouraged me to take. Maybe I could've done both. Maybe not. What I know for sure is this: I never felt like I was sacrificing something. If I had, I wouldn't have been happy, and neither would my family."

Emily sat quietly, absorbing her grandmother's words. "So, you're saying... it's about knowing what feels right for you?"

Ava nodded, her gaze steady. "Exactly. Life puts women at crossroads, Emily–multiple times. Career or family. Passion or stability. Leadership or support. These decisions are tough, but what's most important is that you make them with conviction. If you feel like you're sacrificing a part of yourself, you'll resent it, and that's no way to live."

She paused, taking Emily's hand in hers. "Success isn't one-size-fits-all. For me, it was raising your mom and seeing her thrive. For someone else, it might be running a company or creating art. What matters is that you feel accomplished and fulfilled in what you choose. And that takes determination, no matter the path."

Emily felt a lump form in her throat. "I guess I've been thinking about what kind of future I want, and it's overwhelming. Mom's incredible at balancing everything, and then there's Mrs. Paul, the senator... even the lady who drove me to school today had this amazing story. It feels like there are so many ways to define success, and I'm not sure which one is mine yet."

Ava gave her hand a gentle squeeze. "You don't have to know yet, sweetheart. You're still discovering who you are and what you want. Just promise me one thing: whatever you choose, do it wholeheartedly. Don't let fear or doubt hold you back like it did me. And always remember–you're capable of more than you think."

Emily felt a surge of warmth and clarity as she looked into her grandmother's wise, weathered eyes. "Thank you, Grandma. I'll remember that."

They sat together in silence for a while, watching the sun dip lower in the sky, its golden rays painting the world in soft hues. Emily realized that this conversation, much like the one she'd had with her mother and the professor, was another piece of the puzzle. Each woman in her life was teaching her something unique, helping her build the framework for her own future.

As she stood to leave, Ava called after her with a twinkle in her eye. "Don't forget to tell your mother I gave you the secret to life. She'll love that."

Emily laughed, feeling lighter and more focused than she had in weeks. "I will, Grandma. Thanks for everything."

Riding home, she thought about Ava's words: *Make your choices with conviction.* For the first time, Emily felt less afraid of the crossroads ahead. Whatever path she chose, she would walk it with determination–and with the wisdom of the women who had walked before her.

Your career is your choice – you are in the driving seat

Unexpected Ray of Hope

Social activist discloses shocking past

The warm glow of the ballroom chandeliers reflected off the polished floors as Christy set her empty wine glass on a tray carried by a passing server. The fundraiser had been an overwhelming success, and the buzz of animated conversation filled the air. Christy's mind was still replaying Senator Ramirez's stirring speech when she caught sight of Laura across the room.

Laura, the founder of *Hope for Tomorrow*, stood surrounded by a small group of admirers, her calm yet commanding presence radiating warmth. Christy had worked with Laura through the NGO for years, but tonight, a question lingered in her mind–a curiosity she had never pursued before.

With a confident stride, Christy approached. As the group dispersed, Laura turned and greeted her with a genuine smile. "Christy! It's so good to see you here."

"Likewise, Laura," Christy replied. "I wanted to take a moment to tell you just how incredible this evening has been. The work you've done with *Hope for Tomorrow* is nothing short of transformative."

Laura's smile widened. "Thank you, but it's the team and the community that make it all happen. I'm just a piece of the puzzle."

Christy shook her head. "Don't downplay your role. You've built something extraordinary. And, to be honest, I've always wondered–what inspired you to start all of this? What drives you?"

Laura's expression shifted, her eyes softening as if recalling a distant memory. She gestured toward a quieter corner of the room. "Do you really want to know? It's not exactly a cocktail-party kind of story."

Intrigued, Christy followed her to a small table tucked away from the crowd. The noise of the room faded as Laura began to speak.

"When I was fifteen," Laura started, her voice low but steady, "my entire world fell apart. My parents divorced, and it wasn't the amicable kind. It was ugly, bitter, and destructive. Neither of them had time for me; they were too wrapped up in their own battles. I felt invisible. Unwanted."

Christy leaned forward, her interest piqued. "That must have been so difficult."

"It was," Laura admitted, a shadow passing over her face. "I started hanging out with the wrong crowd—people who didn't judge me, or so I thought. They introduced me to drugs, parties, and a lifestyle that numbed the pain. For a while, it worked. I felt nothing, and nothing felt like peace. But it didn't take long for things to spiral."

Laura's voice trembled slightly as she continued. "At seventeen, I was arrested for possession. I thought that was the end of the line for me. But instead of throwing the book at me, the judge sent me to a recovery home. At first, I hated it. I thought it was a punishment. But it turned out to be my salvation."

Christy's breath caught. She had never imagined Laura's life had begun with such hardship. "What happened at the recovery home?"

"They saw me," Laura said simply, her eyes glistening. "The staff treated me like a person—not a lost cause, not a statistic, but a person with potential. They helped me face my pain, my anger, and my fears. They gave me a second chance, something I hadn't believed I deserved. When I left, I swore to myself that I'd make something of my life."

"And you did," Christy interjected. "You've accomplished so much."

Laura nodded, but there was a bittersweet edge to her smile. "It wasn't immediate. I worked odd jobs, put myself through college, and eventually returned to work at that same recovery home. I stayed there for years, helping kids who were as lost as I had been. That's when I realized my calling–helping children who've been abandoned, neglected, or forgotten. I founded *Hope for Tomorrow* when I was thirty-five, with nothing but a handful of donors and a dream."

Christy felt a lump in her throat. "And look at it now. You've created something incredible. You've turned your pain into purpose."

Laura's gaze was steady. "That's the thing about life, Christy. Sometimes it feels like fate is against us, like the whole world is conspiring to crush us under its weight. And we have two choices: we can let it break us, or we can let it shape us into something stronger. The leader in us has to wake up, take control, and make that decision."

Christy nodded, her mind racing. "It's so easy to get caught up in the setbacks, to feel like there's no way forward."

Laura reached across the table, placing a hand on Christy's arm. "But there is. There's always a way. You just have to find it–and more importantly, believe in it. The decision is yours. Are you going to let life happen to you, or are you going to lead your way through it?"

Christy felt the weight of Laura's words settle in her chest. She thought of her own crossroads, her aspirations to step into the CEO role, and the doubts that sometimes crept into her mind. Laura's story was proof that resilience, determination, and purpose could overcome even the darkest moments.

"Thank you for sharing this with me, Laura," Christy said, her voice thick with emotion. "I think I needed to hear it more than I realized."

Laura smiled warmly. "Sometimes, we all need a little reminder of what we're capable of. Just don't forget to pay it forward."

As Christy left the fundraiser that evening, her mind was alight with inspiration. Laura's journey was a testament to the strength of the human spirit–and a challenge to anyone who dared to dream. Christy knew her path wouldn't be easy, but she felt a renewed determination to face it head-on. And she knew one thing for certain: when the leader within her woke up, there would be no one stopping her.

Failures are inevitable, playing victim never helps. Learn and move on

Neighbor's Counsel

Neighbor is next door, but family is too far.

Emily stepped out of the taxi and paid the driver, still pondering the insights from her conversation with her grandmother. The cool evening air brushed against her face, and as she turned toward the entrance to her home, a cheerful voice stopped her in her tracks.

"Hey, Em! How are you? It's been a while!"

Emily turned to see Mrs. Jane, her neighbor, walking her golden retriever, Max. Jane's radiant smile and impeccable sense of style always struck Emily as effortlessly elegant, but tonight there was an air of calmness around her that Emily found magnetic.

"Hello, Mrs. Jane!" Emily greeted her warmly. "It *has* been a while. How's Max doing?"

Jane chuckled as she patted the dog's head. "Oh, Max is always good company. Keeps me on my toes. How about you? How's college?"

Emily smiled. "It's going great. Just presented a paper today, actually. Quite a learning experience."

Jane's eyes lit up. "Good for you, Emily! You're such a bright young woman–I'm sure you nailed it."

As they stood under the streetlight, their conversation shifted to the tranquility of their neighborhood—the quiet streets, the leafy trees that lined the sidewalks, and the way the world seemed to slow down in this pocket of the city. It wasn't long before Emily's curiosity about Jane's personal life got the better of her.

"Mrs. Jane, I've always wondered," Emily began hesitantly, "I never see your family around. Do they live here?"

Jane's smile softened, and she leaned back slightly, as if bracing herself for a familiar question. "Ah, no, my husband and kids live in San Francisco."

"San Francisco?" Emily echoed, her surprise evident. "But you're here in New York. How does that work?"

Jane shifted Max's leash to her other hand and nodded. "It's a bit unconventional, I'll admit. My husband, Greg, and I had to make a tough decision a few years ago when I was promoted to Chief Strategy Officer at my company. The job required me to relocate to the headquarters here in New York."

Emily blinked. "That must've been a huge adjustment—for everyone."

"It was," Jane admitted, "but it was a conscious decision. Greg and I talked about it endlessly before I made the move. He's an architect, and his projects are all based in San Francisco. The kids were already settled there with their school and friends. Uprooting everyone didn't make sense, and they all supported me in pursuing this opportunity."

Emily couldn't help but admire Jane's candidness. "Did you ever feel like you were sacrificing something? Being away from them, I mean?"

Jane tilted her head thoughtfully. "You know, that's an interesting question. A lot of people—especially women—frame these choices as sacrifices. And it's true, I miss my family every single day. But I don't see it as a sacrifice. I see it as a step forward. If men can relocate for work and have their families support them without it being called a sacrifice, why can't we?"

Emily absorbed the wisdom in Jane's words, her mind racing. "That's such a powerful perspective. I've never thought about it that way."

Jane smiled gently. "It's all about mindset, Em. Women often self-sympathize—we start seeing our choices through a lens of guilt and loss, even when we're doing something that fulfills us. But here's the thing: guilt gets you nowhere. Determination does. My family and I made this decision together, and because of that, I don't feel like I'm alone or that I'm sacrificing anything. They're my rock."

Emily nodded slowly, impressed by Jane's clarity. "I guess it's about finding that balance–making sure your decisions align with your goals while also keeping your family in the loop."

"Exactly," Jane said, her tone firm but encouraging. "And here's the secret: when you stop treating your career as something you have to apologize for, the people around you–your family, your colleagues, even your friends–start respecting it too. It's a shift in perspective, and it makes all the difference."

Max barked, tugging at his leash, and Jane laughed. "Looks like Max thinks I'm getting too philosophical."

Emily grinned. "Not at all. This has been really inspiring. I've been thinking a lot about career paths and leadership lately, and what you've said tonight really resonates."

Jane placed a hand on Emily's shoulder. "You're young, Emily, and you have the world ahead of you. But remember this—no matter what path you choose, own it. Whether it's your career, your family, or something entirely different, don't let the world make you feel small for your choices. You'll find that when you stand firm, the people who matter will stand with you."

Emily felt a surge of determination rise within her. She watched as Jane and Max disappeared down the street, the weight of their conversation settling in her mind like a puzzle piece clicking into place.

As she walked toward her door, Emily found herself repeating Jane's words. **Own your path. Don't apologize for it.** The phrase echoed in her thoughts like a mantra, fueling her resolve. She wasn't just inspired; she was ready to lead her own way—on her terms.

" Most times life puts you through tough challenges, never hesitate to seek support from family and friends by staying strong and steady"

New Reflection

Silent Drive Sound Mind

The car's engine hummed softly as Christy navigated the quiet streets, the dim glow of the dashboard lights casting a serene ambiance. The day had been long, but as she drove home, her thoughts played back the tapestry of conversations she had been a part of. Each interaction was like a vivid scene from a movie–voices, expressions, and words interwoven with wisdom, admiration, and encouragement.

Her mind lingered on Senator Ramirez's powerful anecdotes about resilience and influence in politics. The senator's words had been clear and unwavering: "You've built something remarkable, Christy. Don't let the challenges you face dim the light you carry."

Then there was Laura, with her harrowing yet transformative story of redemption. Laura's voice echoed in her thoughts: "You've shown that leadership isn't about having all the answers; it's about creating paths for others. That's a rare gift."

And, of course, the simplicity of Clara's humility and hard work. Christy smiled as she remembered Clara's warm laugh and modest pride. "You've always been a role model for me, Christy," Clara had said.

"If I've climbed up, it's because I watched how you led."

She had spent so much time second-guessing herself, worrying about whether she was good enough to reach for the next rung of the ladder, that she had missed the obvious: she was already inspiring people. To her team, to her peers, and even to strangers who crossed her path, Christy was a symbol of strength and balance. But there was one person she had failed to inspire—herself.

Her phone buzzed on the passenger seat. She glanced at it quickly and saw Emily's name flash across the screen. The thought of her daughter warmed her heart. Emily had called twice today, asking probing questions and seeking guidance—questions Christy knew came from Emily's desire to understand the world and her place in it. **Emily looked up to her.** That alone was proof that she was capable of achieving anything she set her sights on.

She pulled over to the side of the road, the sound of crickets filling the quiet night. Her reflection in the rearview mirror caught her eye. The faintest hint of a tear glistened, but her expression was one of determination.

Christy's lips curved into a smile. Emily's question that morning had been the seed that started it all: **"Why do we have so few female CEOs in the world?"** That seemingly simple query had unraveled layers of self-reflection throughout the day. How had she not seen the obvious until now? Emily wasn't just asking about the world; she was asking about her. Christy could see it now—Emily's hunger for answers, for inspiration, for permission to dream bigger.

She turned into her neighborhood, the familiar streets lined with quiet houses and dim porch lights. The car slowed as Christy's thoughts gained momentum. A question simmered in her mind, sharp and insistent: **"Why have I waited so long?"**

She thought about a statement Jane had made earlier that day. **"You've got to own your path, Christy. Stop apologizing for being ambitious. You inspire people when you embrace who you are fully."**

Christy leaned back in her seat, letting the words settle deep in her mind. **When had she stopped believing in herself?** Maybe it was during the sleepless nights juggling deadlines and Emily's homework. Or the moments she faced in boardrooms full of skepticism because she was the only woman at the table. Or the rare nights when she wondered if she could truly balance it all.

The truth was, she hadn't lost belief entirely–she had just let doubt creep in. And that doubt had become a silent passenger, whispering questions that made her hesitate.

For too long, she had let self-doubt and fear of failure dictate her choices. She had internalized the idea that to be bold was to be reckless, that to assert herself too much might tarnish the respect she had earned. But today had shown her something profound: every person she had spoken to saw her as more than capable–as a leader, a mentor, and a source of inspiration.

Christy's thoughts sharpened, her vision clear as she stared ahead at the empty road. **"Be an inspiration to others by being an inspiration to yourself."** It wasn't just a platitude; it was a way forward. She couldn't lead if she didn't believe in her ability to rise above the noise of doubt. She couldn't light the way for others if her own fire was dim.

The road stretched out before her, like a metaphor for what lay ahead. Her journey wasn't over. There were new challenges to face, new heights to climb, and new lessons to learn. But now, she carried a renewed conviction: **She was enough. She was capable. She was ready.**

Christy felt her grip on the wheel was firm and steady. The headlights cut through the darkness, illuminating the path ahead. As she drove home, the words of everyone she had spoken to that day seemed to merge into a singular thought: **"You've got to believe in yourself to make the world believe in you."**

Deeply involved in her own thinking, Christy reached home before she could realize. She stepped out of the car, the night air crisp against her skin. As she walked to the front door, another phrase surfaced in her thoughts, one that encapsulated the day's lessons: **"Be an inspiration to others by being an inspiration to yourself."**

It wasn't a cliché–it was a call to action. She needed to stop waiting for permission, for validation, for the stars to align. **Leadership wasn't about being perfect; it was about showing up, owning your strengths, and pushing forward despite the challenges.**

Inside, the house was quiet, Emily was wide awake waiting. Christy set her keys on the counter and poured herself a glass of water. The reflection in the kitchen window caught her eye, and for the first time in a long while, she didn't see a woman weighed down by expectations. She saw someone ready to rise above them.

Her thoughts circled back to the day's central theme: breaking perceptions, moving beyond opinions, and embracing her own potential. **It wasn't too late. It was never too late.**

As she climbed the stairs to her room, a new energy coursed through her veins. She didn't have all the answers, and there were no guarantees. But one thing was clear: she was done waiting. The world wouldn't believe in her until she believed in herself.

Tonight, she wasn't just inspired–she was resolved.

"Remember! Inspiring yourself is the most important step of all."

Shared Epiphany

The day ends a new chapter begins

Christy descended the staircase slowly, her hand gliding along the smooth banister. There was a lightness in her step that hadn't been there in years. It wasn't just the thrill of a good day or the satisfaction of meaningful conversations–it was the sense of having peeled back a layer of herself she hadn't even realized was there.

As she reached the bottom step, her eyes fell on Emily, sprawled on the couch, scrolling through her phone. There was something different about her, too. Emily's face was lit not just by the glow of the screen but by a quiet, radiant energy. When Emily looked up, their eyes met, and for a moment, there was a shared understanding between them–a connection that transcended words.

"Hey, Mom," Emily said, sitting up. "You look... different. Lighter, maybe?"

Christy chuckled as she walked over to join her. "Funny you say that. I was just thinking the same about you."

Emily grinned. "Maybe it's contagious."

They both laughed, a sound that felt unburdened, almost therapeutic. It wasn't often that their conversations felt this charged with positivity and purpose. Sure, they talked daily—about schedules, errands, grades—but this felt different. It was as if the day had granted them both a fresh perspective.

"So," Emily began, tucking her legs beneath her. "I had the most amazing conversations today. With Mrs. Jane, with Mrs. Paul, even with a stranger—Helga, my cab driver. It's like... everyone had something profound to say."

Christy leaned forward, intrigued. "Helga? That's an interesting name. What did she say?"

Emily recounted the story of the cab driver who had rebuilt her life after tragedy, and how she managed to balance her responsibilities as a single mother with her career. Christy listened intently, nodding as Emily spoke.

"It made me realize," Emily concluded, "there's so much wisdom in the people around us. We just need to pay attention."

Christy smiled, feeling a deep sense of pride. "You're absolutely right. And you know what's funny? I've been thinking the same thing all day. From Senator Ramirez to Laura and even Jane next door, I kept hearing stories that reminded me of how much inspiration is right under our noses. It's like the universe was trying to send me a message."

Emily tilted her head, curious. "What message?"

"That we've been so focused on looking forward–our goals, our challenges, our ambitions–that we've forgotten to look around," Christy said. "There's a wealth of knowledge, resilience, and strength in the people we interact with every day. And we can learn so much if we just take the time to listen."

Emily's eyes sparkled with understanding. "That's exactly what I felt today! Like, all these people have been around me forever, but I never noticed how much they had to teach me. Mrs. Paul's advice about seeking feedback, Jane's perspective on sacrifice, even Helga's grit... it's all just there, waiting to be noticed."

They sat in companionable silence for a moment, each lost in thought. Then Christy pulled out her phone and opened a blank note.

"What are you doing?" Emily asked.

"Making a list," Christy said, tapping away. "Of everything we learned today. Let's capture it before we forget."

Emily grabbed her own phone, excited. "Oh, that's a great idea! Okay, let's start with this: 'Confidence comes from within, but feedback refines it.' That's Mrs. Paul's."

Christy nodded, adding her own entry. "And here's one: 'Leadership is about making choices, not excuses.' That's from Jane."

They went back and forth, listing every nugget of wisdom they'd gleaned throughout the day. With each entry, they felt a deeper sense of amazement–not just at the insights themselves but at the realization that they'd been surrounded by these lessons all along. They named it Ready Reckoner for Success.

When they finally looked up from their phones, the list was long, but their faces were brighter.

"This is incredible," Emily said, her voice tinged with awe. "We've learned more in one day than I thought possible."

Christy reached over and squeezed her daughter's hand. "And the best part? This is just the beginning. If we stay open–really open–we'll keep learning, every single day."

Emily nodded, her expression thoughtful. "You know, Mom, I've been thinking... A lot of people seem to get stuck because they're waiting for the 'right time' to make a choice. But maybe the right time is just whenever you decide it is."

Christy smiled, her heart swelling with pride. "Exactly, Em. Any woman can choose to be whatever she wants to be. But it starts with making that choice. And once you make it, you have to own it–completely."

The two of them sat there, basking in the warmth of their shared epiphany. The future felt wide open, full of promise and possibility. For the first time in a long while, they weren't just mother and daughter–they were allies, companions on a journey of growth and self-discovery.

As the clock struck midnight, Christy glanced at Emily and said, "You know what? The future looks bright."

Emily smiled, a glint of determination in her eyes. "Brighter than ever."

It is rather clear now that it is not just one CEO in the making may be two but why not three, You?

Did Christy make it? How did Emily shape her future? Coming Soon!

Ready Reckoner for Success

Frequent Introspection

Perception Management

Courage and Determination

Decision Making

Understand the importance of Purpose

Challenges will keep coming

Know your Strength

More important to know your limitations

Learning is Growth

Hard Work

Resilience

Find your calling

Your Life is your choice

Take charge of your career

Accountability is key

Seek Support

Face failure to learn

It is never too late

Success is not easy but always possible